Smithsonian

SUPER SCIENCE ACTIVITY BOOK

Silver Dolphin

Smithsonian SUPER SCIENCE ACTIVITY BOOK

Silver Dolphin Books
An imprint of Printers Row Publishing Group
A division of Readerlink Distribution Services, LLC
10350 Barnes Canyon Road, Suite 100, San Diego, CA 92121
www.silverdolphinbooks.com

ISBN: 978-1-68412-055-0

Manufactured, printed, and assembled in China.
First printing, January 2017.

21 20 19 18 17 1 2 3 4 5

Written by Steve Behling and Rachel Bozek
Designed by Creative Giant Puzzles and Games
Reviewed by Kealy Gordon and Ellen Nanney

For Smithsonian Enterprises:
Kealy Gordon, Product Development Manager, Licensing
Ellen Nanney, Licensing Manager
Brigid Ferraro, Vice President, Education and Consumer Products
Carol LeBlanc, Senior Vice President, Education and Consumer Products
Chris Liedel, President

Image Credits:
Thinkstock, NASA, John Francis, Franco Tempesta, Creative Giant Inc.

Every effort has been made to contact copyright holders for the images in this book. If you are the copyright holder of any uncredited image herein, please contact us at Silver Dolphin Books, 10350 Barnes Canyon Road, Suite 100, San Diego, CA 92121.

CONTENTS

JUNGLE JAM

Deep in the forest, soaring trees rise up from the forest floor. Bright flowers grow from the trees, and snakes coil over branches. Noisy monkeys scamper through the treetops as colorful birds fly from branch to branch. Just one small stretch of rainforest may be home to hundreds of species!

A lush, green tangle of trees and vines forms the tropical rainforest. The combination of warm temperatures and lots of rainfall makes this jungle a place that supports all types of plant, animal, and insect life.

EQUATOR

● = TROPICAL RAINFORESTS

WILD WONDER!

Only 6 percent of the earth is rainforest, but almost half of the planet's plants and animals call it home.

IN THE SHADOWS!

You'll need the **STICKERS** at the end of the book.

Match the stickers to the shadows ... but look closely! Not every shadow has a matching sticker!

Answers on page 94.

5

BENEATH THE SURFACE

Prairie dogs are rodents, a bit larger than ground squirrels. They are very social animals that live in huge underground burrows, called towns. Prairie dog families are called coteries. Each coterie has entrances to their burrow that they guard from other coteries.

Home:
Western North America

Prairie dogs are herbivores. They like to eat grasses, roots, and seeds.

WILD WONDER!

Alert! Prairie dog predators include hawks, eagles, coyotes, and snakes. When a prairie dog first sees a predator, it will give a sharp warning call, known as a "bark," to warn others of danger.

OPERATION UNDERGROUND!

START!

Help this
PRARIE DOG
travel deep
into her
burrow!

FINISH!

OUT OF THE ORDINARY

Many animal species have unique characteristics that make them remarkable. Here are just a few that are particularly unusual—and interesting!

Axolotl

Dugong

Narwhal

Cassowary

Arapaima

Capybara

WILD WONDER!
Growing to about 4 and a half feet long, the capybara is the world's largest rodent.

Pika

Sloth

Scientists estimate that there are nearly eight million different animal species on our planet, but less than a million have been described and cataloged. That means there are millions more animals yet to be discovered and described.

Kit fox

Red panda

Kinkajou

Glass frog

Platypus

River dolphin

ON A WORD SEARCH!

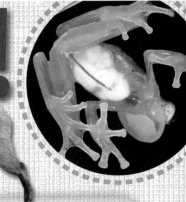

Many animals are hard to find in the wild, but even harder to find in this puzzle! Find the words at the bottom of the page in the grid below. Words can be hidden up and down, backward and forward, and diagonally.

```
H V X D Q D K N V Q Y Y Q H V
C T D N I E Z U H P A N E D T
J A O J K U E N L N I A X K Y
R V S L S O Y A T H G E P H J
E A P S S U T L P X O F T I K
D U R C O Y G L A S S F R O G
P O T A P W O A M I A P A R A
A J P U B D A S N K Q Y P W X
N A S Q R Y U R I A H N X O O
D K K E E P P P Y K R D T A L
A N V M Y C F A V I U W X H O
G I N T P I C A C G V U H S T
R K L U W J Q U O H Y S L A L
X A R E D P A N N A L I N A L
P I C D T Q G B X Y Z K Z N A
```

pika	**red panda**	**narwhal**	**capybara**
dugong	**sloth**	**axolotl**	**cassowary**
kit fox	**platypus**	**arapaima**	**kinkajou**
glass frog	**river dolphin**		

Answers on page 94.

AMAZING ARACHNIDS

Scorpions are arachnids, so they are related to spiders. Scorpions are unique among arachnids because they have two pincers and a long, curled-up, stinger-tipped tail.

There are nearly 2,000 species of scorpions, ranging from half an inch to eight inches long.

The bark scorpion is the biggest scorpion in the United States and has the most powerful venom.

WILD WONDER!
Ultraviolet light causes the scorpion to glow, probably to attract its meal of insects at night.

Some brave people keep SCORPIONS as pets!

SPOT THE SCORPION!

Only one of the scorpions below matches the one here. Can you spot the one that's the same?

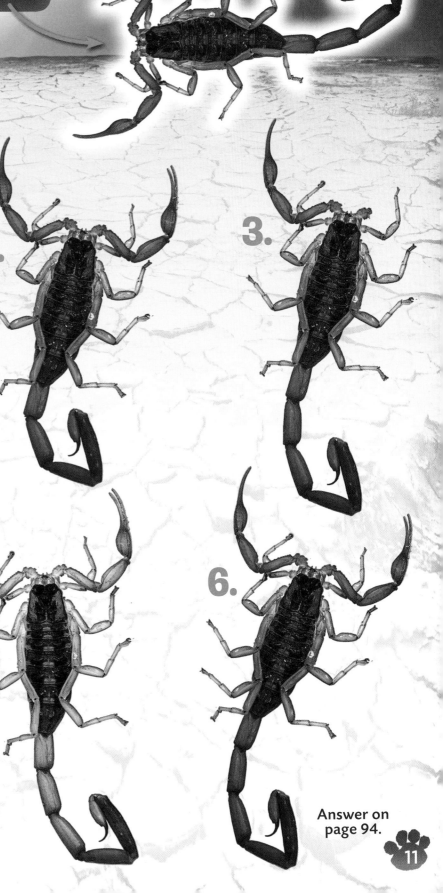

1.

2.

3.

4.

5.

6.

Answer on page 94.

11

WORLD OF WINGS

In the rainforest, the understory is the area that stretches from below the canopy's branches to the forest floor. Fluttering through the rainforest's understory are dozens of species of butterflies and moths.

GIANT ATLAS MOTH

Butterflies and moths help pollinate flowers. Pollination is what helps plants reproduce. These insects often have long, tubular mouths. They insert these into flowers to sip their nectar. While they do this, pollen from the flower sticks to their bodies and wings. They carry this pollen from flower to flower, pollinating plants along the way!

CANOPY

UNDERSTORY

FOREST FLOOR

MALACHITE BUTTERFLY

AGRIAS BUTTERFLY

BLUE MORPHO BUTTERFLY

WILD WONDER!
Butterflies are usually active during the day, while moths are typically nocturnal.

MADAGASCAR MOON MOTH

DOODLE·A·BUG!

DOODLING!

Draw a scene that includes beautiful butterflies and moths in the space provided.

EXPLORING THE SAVANNA

The savanna is a dry grassland that has warm temperatures all year round and usually only gets rain in the summers. There are grasses, a few scattered trees, and lots of different animal species that make their home here.

Lions are the only cats to live in social groups, and these groups are called prides. A pride is made up of female lions, their cubs, and either one or a few male lions that are brothers. The lionesses are faster than the male lions and provide the pride with food they've hunted.

Gazelles are a type of antelope. They run fast and can outrun predators over long distances.

Because they're so big, giraffes can't easily hide from predators on the wide-open savanna. When they band together, their spotted coats make it hard for predators to pick out a single giraffe.

Elephants live in close groups, called herds, made up of mothers and their babies, called calves. The mothers band together to protect the calves by charging and swinging their tusks.

Of the three species of hyenas (spotted, brown, and striped), the spotted is the largest. They're fast, they travel in packs, and the sound they make can be mistaken for laughter.

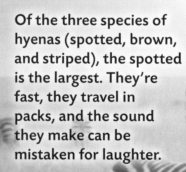

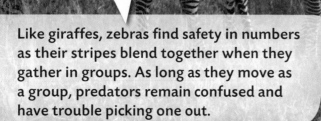

Like giraffes, zebras find safety in numbers as their stripes blend together when they gather in groups. As long as they move as a group, predators remain confused and have trouble picking one out.

STRIPES GALORE!

How many zebras can you find?

Chameleons: Masters of
CAMOUFLAGE

Each chameleon species can change the color and pattern of its skin in a different way. Chameleons do this as a way to communicate with each other. Their colors can change depending on the temperature, the amount of light, and even on their mood.

They like to eat insects such as locusts, grasshoppers, and crickets. The smallest chameleon species is less than an inch long, while the largest can grow to be nearly two feet.

WILD WONDER!
Chameleons live in Asia, Africa, Madagascar, Spain, and Portugal.

COLOR, COLOR, COLOR, COLOR, COLOR
CHAMELEONS!

Help these chameleons communicate by giving them bright and beautiful colors and patterns.

WILD WONDER!

Chameleons have four layers of skin, each with different colors. Nerve impulses and hormone changes cause the skin cells to shrink and expand. Blending the different layers of skin creates unique colors and patterns.

A WHALE OF A DOLPHIN

ORCAS are toothed whales. Their strong, cone-shaped teeth allow them to bite down and hold onto prey.

Orcas are the largest of all the dolphin species. They travel and hunt in family groups called pods. The pods work together to hunt food and protect their young.

Orcas make themselves at home in cold, coastal waters from the North and South Poles to the equator. They eat fish, seabirds, and marine mammals, including seals and sea lions.

WILD WONDER!

Pod members have their own way of communicating with one another. In fact, each orca family has unique sounds that help its members identify and call out to other family members.

ORCA BELOW!

CONNECT THE DOTS from 1 to 172, then shade in the areas with the letter "O" to complete your orca!

START

Male orcas have triangular dorsal fins that can be up to six feet tall. Female orcas have curved dorsal fins that are only about three feet tall.

Orcas' eyes are just below their white eye patches.

Pectoral fins are used for turning.

Whales and dolphins, including orcas, swim by moving their powerful tail, or fluke, up and down. Fish, including sharks, swim by moving their tail from side to side.

As it reaches the water's surface, an orca exhales air out of a single blowhole on the top of its head.

DESERT DWELLERS

Camels are well suited for desert life: they have long legs to keep them high above the hot sand, hair in their ears to block blowing sand, and a double row of eyelashes and inner eyelids to keep the sand out of their eyes. And they can close their nostrils!

WILD WONDER!

A camel's hump doesn't actually store water—it's filled with fatty tissue. The camel uses the fat as a food supply and can also draw water from the fat.

Dromedaries, the one-humped camels, live in North Africa and the Middle East. Bactrian camels, the two-humped kind, live in Central Asia.

Most four-legged animals walk by moving one front leg at the same time as the back leg on the opposite side. But camels (as well as giraffes and bears) move both legs on one side of their body at a time. Then they move both legs on the other side. This is called pacing.

COMPLETE THE CAMEL!

Draw the other half of this Bactrian camel.

FEELING DESERTED

What do you think is going through this camel's head out there in the deserts of Central Asia?

YOU ARE HERE

The Milky Way consists of hundreds of billions of stars—our Sun included. The Milky Way galaxy spans about 100,000 light-years across.

To humans, the **Milky Way** is the most important galaxy in the universe because it is the one we live in. But it is actually just one among billions of spiral-shaped galaxies in the universe.

Galactic Longitide
0°

75,000 ly

30°

330°

60,000 ly

Perseus Arm

OUR SOLAR SYSTEM

Scutum–Centaurus Arm

45,000 ly

Galactic Bar

Long Bar

60°

Far 3kpc Arm

300°

Near 3kpc Arm

Sagittarius Arm

Outer Arm

90°

Orion Spur

Sun

270°

Norma Arm

15,000 ly

THE SUN is the center of our solar system. In our solar system, eight planets orbit the Sun. Keep on reading to find out more about them!

30,000 ly

150°

180°

210°

FAR-OUT FACT!

If you find a place with a very dark night sky, you can observe the Milky Way as an outstretched streak of white light, filled with dust, gas clouds, and twinkling stars. Ancient people saw it too, and they referred to our galaxy as a path, as a river, and as milk.

CONNECT THE
CONSTELLATIONS!

For thousands of years, people have used star patterns, called constellations, to mark the passage of time. The arrangement of stars in the sky doesn't change, but their location and position change throughout the year as Earth travels around the Sun.

Take a look at the constellations in the boxes to the left. Then find them in the sky below. Can you connect the stars to make Ursa Minor, Ursa Major, and Cassiopeia?

Ursa Major

Cassiopeia

Ursa Minor

THE SUN

The Sun is a hot star and the star of our solar system. The gravitational pull of the Sun is what holds our solar system together.

The Sun is made mostly of two elements: helium and hydrogen. The force of gravity squeezes the gasses into a hot ball and turns the helium into hydrogen. This chemical reaction is what makes the Sun give out heat and light.

The size of the Sun compared to Earth

1 Earth

The Sun's diameter is about 100 times that of Earth, so it would take 100 Earths, end to end, to stretch across the diameter of the Sun.

FAR-OUT FACT!

The Sun is much larger than Earth. You could fit one million Earths inside the Sun! So ... it's big!

HOT STUFF!

We just told you that the Sun is hot. How hot?
Take the quiz below to see if you can guess which is hotter!

Which is hotter?
The Sun or...

1. ... Venus?
   a) The Sun
   b) Venus

2. ... a really hot stove?
   a) The Sun
   b) A really hot stove

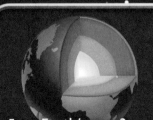

3. ... molten lava?
   a) The Sun
   b) Molten lava

4. ... a laser beam?
   a) The Sun
   b) A laser beam

5. ... Earth's core?
   a) The Sun
   b) Earth's core

Answers on page 94.

MERCURY AND VENUS

Mercury is the closest planet to the Sun, and it has the smallest orbit around that body—it completes a revolution around the Sun in only 88 Earth days. By comparison, the Earth completes a revolution around the Sun in approximately 365 days.

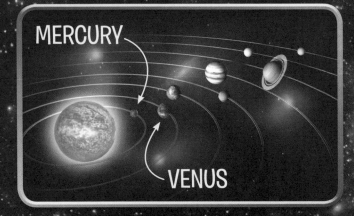

MERCURY

VENUS

FAR-OUT FACT!

Even though Mercury is the closest planet to the Sun, it's not the hottest. That honor goes to Venus, because of its carbon dioxide atmosphere.

Venus is the second planet from the Sun, and the closest planet to Earth. The planet's air is full of deadly acid and is scorching hot: hot enough to melt lead!

MESSENGER ON THE MOVE!

See if you can help the *Messenger* space probe navigate through our solar system, past Venus, before arriving at Mercury! Here are the rules.

1. Blasting off from **Earth**, move one circle at a time in any direction along the pathways.

2. Blue circles can move to blue or green circles. Red circles can move to red or green circles. Green circles can move to blue or red circles. NO COLOR CAN MOVE TO A YELLOW CIRCLE.

3. You must get to **Venus** first. After Venus, continue on.

4. Land on **Mercury** to finish your mission!

MESSENGER

EARTH

MERCURY

VENUS

EARTH

Earth's Moon may be small, but it's strong. As the Moon revolves around our planet, its gravity pulls Earth and the water on Earth toward it. This gravitational pull actually creates the high and low tides of our oceans.

Can you name the third planet from the Sun and the amazing home planet of more than 30 million different forms of life? If you guessed Earth, you guessed right.

Earth is protected by its atmosphere, which gives us the air we breathe. It also acts as a buffer that protects us from meteorites, and it blocks out deadly radiation.

EARTH

FAR-OUT FACT!

Reset your clocks! The length of a typical day on planet Earth is actually 23 hours, 56 minutes.

SUIT UP!

Step into outer space for even a minute, and you're going to need a spacesuit! Spacesuits provide a pressurized atmosphere, breathable oxygen, controlled temperatures, and protection for astronauts from flying debris.

Design your own protective spacesuit in the space below.

THE FIRST MARTIAN

Fill in the word balloon above with what you might say if you were the first person on Mars!

An **astronaut** is someone who is trained to travel in spacecraft.

MARS

The fourth planet from the Sun, Mars, is known as the "Red Planet." That's because it has a lot of iron in its soil and the air on Mars has caused the iron to rust.

MARS

Scientists think that billions of years ago, Mars may have been warmer and wetter, almost like Earth. But over time, Mars's atmosphere became thinner, and conditions on the planet became much colder.

FAR-OUT FACT!

Mars is easier to study than Venus or Mercury. We can see Mars's surface from Earth using a telescope.

The dry Martian surface gets churned up by winds, creating massive dust storms that cover the planet and can rage for more than a month.

MARS MAZE!

Scientists use rovers, motorized vehicles that take pictures and conduct tests, to learn more about Mars. They want to explore Mars because the discovery of water there has led scientists to believe that it may have once been more like Earth. Can you guide the Mars rover to find water? Watch out for mountains and volcanoes!

START!

FINISH!

JUPITER AND SATURN

The most massive planet in the solar system is Jupiter. The fifth planet from the Sun, Jupiter is called a gas giant—the planet does not have a solid surface.

JUPITER

SATURN

FAR-OUT FACT!

Which planet has more moons—Jupiter or Saturn? The honor goes to Jupiter, with at least 67 moons. Saturn has at least 62 known moons.

Saturn, the sixth planet from the Sun, has a ring system made up of seven individual rings that have gaps between them. The rings are named A through G, in the order in which they were discovered.

WAY-OUT WORDS!

See if you can find the names of some of Saturn's moons in the grid below. When you're done, try finding the names of the *eight planets in our solar system*, too! Words can be hidden up and down, backward and forward, and diagonally.

Tethys
Dione
Janus
Epimethius
Titan
Hyperion
Iapetus

```
E C R E S C I I Y R U C R E M
N P F E N U A A S T H X S D H
U Z I Q T P N Z B W F Y U I T
T D E M E I P E V Z H K Z O R
P S N T E K P K V T Y Q I N A
E J U R U T L U E A P F R E E
N S Z D B R H T J R E R I Y B
S A T U R N A I P L R W J N S
N A T I T L D N U L I F V R Q
W G D Y S T J W U S O B A K R
L W B A R A K U R S N M D Z P
E I V C N U H P X C L X Y N S
V I E U S F C B M V R M G V B
P M S O Q K H R H X V E I H L
```

URANUS AND NEPTUNE

Mars may be the red planet, but Uranus is… the green pea? That's what the seventh planet from the Sun looks like when viewed through a telescope. Uranus is eight times larger than Earth!

URANUS

NEPTUNE

Neptune is the eighth planet from the Sun, so it's extremely cold, and it is the farthest planet ever reached by spacecraft. In 1989, 12 years after leaving Earth, *Voyager 2* passed by Neptune.

FAR-OUT FACT!

Though Neptune may be farther away from the Sun, Uranus is the coldest planet in the solar system. It has the lowest recorded temperature of -366°F.

ORDER UP!

Put the planets from our solar system around the Sun in the correct order!

You'll need the **STICKERS** at the end of the book.

We received a deep-space message from Pluto asking to be included. **SORRY, PLUTO!** You're not a planet anymore!

SEEING INTO SPACE

Launched in 1990, the Hubble Space Telescope orbits Earth and is the first major optical telescope placed in space. It has changed the way we view the universe. Hubble has captured thousands of images and has illuminated faraway galaxies, stars, and much more!

Hubble wears corrective lenses, like people do when they wear eyeglasses. So far, the Hubble Telescope has taken more than 1.2 million observations.

Hubble is about the size of a school bus, but it's much faster than a typical school bus, orbiting at a speed of 17,000 miles per hour!

SCHOOL BUS

Every 97 minutes, Hubble completes an orbit around Earth. It has orbited Earth more than 110,000 TIMES since 1990.

SPACE SELFIE!

DOODLING!

NASA's Hubble is famous for taking stunning images of distant planets, stars, nebulae, and galaxies. Draw a colorful galactic picture that the Hubble could capture.

(Be sure to include yourself in the scene—it is a selfie, after all!)

SPACE I O TABLET

WORKING IN SPACE

A space station is a piloted satellite built to remain in low orbit around Earth for a long time. Most space stations can act as a dock for spacecraft. Space stations allow scientists to study the effects of long-term spaceflight on the human body.

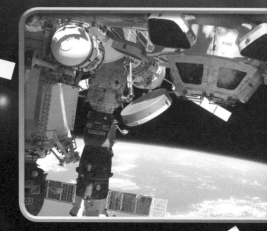

Space stations also allow for extended scientific studies, where crews can be rotated in and out, with each crew member staying aboard the station for weeks or months.

FAR-OUT FACT!
Skylab was the United States' first space station, and orbited Earth from 1973 until 1979.

The first crew arrived at the International Space Station (ISS) in 2000. The ISS was built so that astronauts from all over the world could visit and learn about space. It's so large that at certain times, it can be seen from Earth without a telescope.

ASTRONAUTS WANTED!

Do you want to live and work aboard a space station? Fill out our astronaut application and see if you have the right stuff!

FORM #NASA071821

OFFICIAL ASTRONAUT APPLICATION

NAME: _____

AGE: _____

HOMETOWN: _____

MY FAVORITE PLANET IS:

_____

SPACE STATION SPECIALTY (CHOOSE ONE)

[   ] Scientist   [   ] Pilot

[   ] Payload specialist   [   ] Spacewalk specialist

[   ] WRITE YOUR OWN: _____

_____

I WANT TO BE AN ASTRONAUT BECAUSE...

_____

_____

_____

_____

_____

GLUE
your photo
here!

A BONE TO PICK

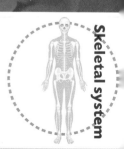

Skeletal system

The adult human skeleton is made up of 206 bones. Bones help you move and give you shape.

The adult spine is made up of 26 ring-shaped bones called vertebrae. You can feel your spine in the center of your back—those bumps are your vertebrae!

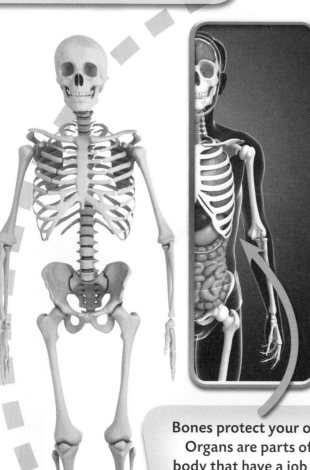

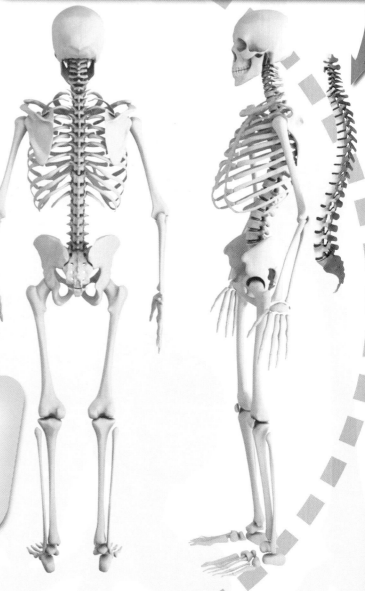

Bones protect your organs. Organs are parts of the body that have a job to do. Ribs are bones that protect your lungs and heart. Your skull protects your brain.

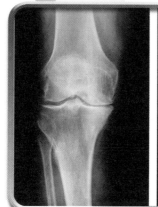

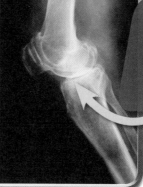

BODY OF TRUTH!

A joint is where two bones come together. Joints let you move, bend, and twist.

BODY WORK!

This skeleton is missing half of its body! Draw the other half.

The human skull is made up of 22 bones.

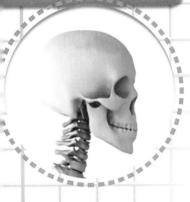

The three smallest bones in your body are all in the ear. The smallest is called the stapes.

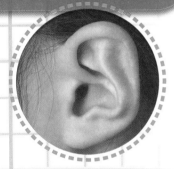

Each human hand has 27 bones, while each foot has 26.

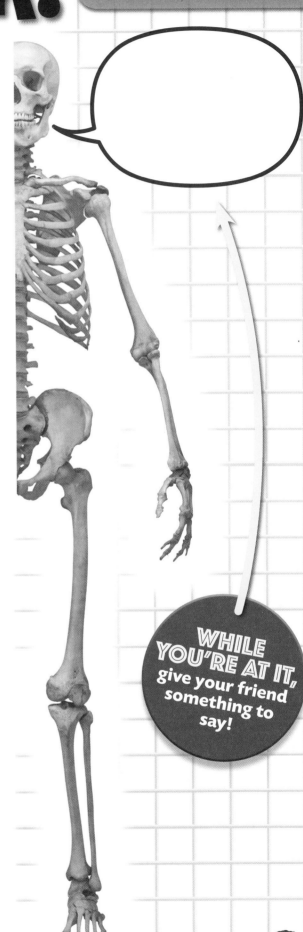

WHILE YOU'RE AT IT, give your friend something to say!

WASTEFUL THINKING

Your blood flows from the small intestines to your liver. The liver decides how much food to store. It also decides how much food to send through the body. Finally, the liver gets rid of waste, which it sends to your large intestine.

Kidneys get rid of waste in the blood, too. The waste mixes with water. Then the waste is stored in your bladder. You get rid of that when you go to the bathroom.

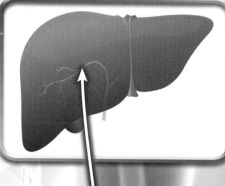

KIDNEYS

BLADDER

ESOPHAGUS

LIVER

STOMACH

GALLBLADDER

SPLEEN

SMALL INTESTINE

PANCREAS

APPENDIX

LARGE INTESTINE

BODY OF TRUTH!
Your small intestine is actually longer than your large intestine, but your large intestine is much wider.

LAST STOP: LARGE INTESTINE!

The large and small intestines are important parts of your digestive system. Your large intestine absorbs water and is the last stop for waste before it leaves your body. Help the waste get through the small intestine and then all the way to the end of the large intestine!

START!

FINISH!

STRENGTH IN NUMBERS

Muscular system

The human body has about 650 muscles. Smooth muscles work in hollow organs, such as your stomach. They push food through your body and work when you don't even know they're working!

BODY OF TRUTH!
The cardiac muscle is your heart. It works on its own, pumping blood through your body.

You control your skeletal muscles, which are connected to your bones and help form your shape.

THE EYES HAVE IT!

Stare closely at the yellow dot in the image below for one minute. Then look at a blank wall, blink a few times, and see how a negative of the picture has stayed in your view for a short time after you look away!

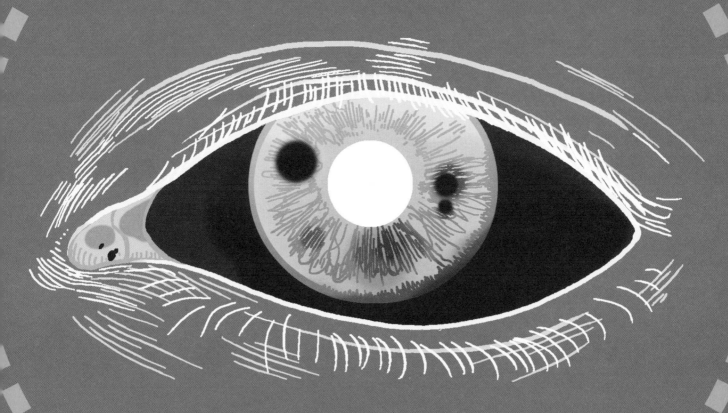

Each of your **EYEBALLS** is controlled by six muscles in its socket.

Your retina contains cells, called rods and cones, which help your brain figure out what you're looking at. Rods help you see when there's not a lot of light, and cones help you identify colors.

45

OPEN YOUR MOUTH

Muscular system

The human body makes two sets of teeth. Your baby teeth take about three years to grow. After a few years, baby teeth are pushed out by adult teeth. Teeth are important for chewing, talking, and singing.

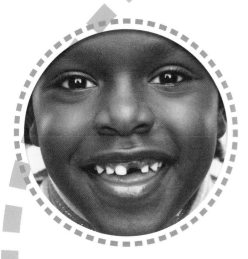

BODY OF TRUTH!
There are between 2,000 and 5,000 taste buds on the front and back of your tongue. And still more in the rest of your mouth!

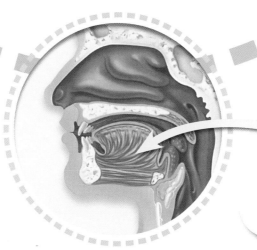

In addition to chewing, talking, and singing, the tongue also tastes food. It helps you swallow the food you chew. And the tongue fights germs. You can move your tongue because it has many muscles.

TIME TO EAT!

DOODLING!

DRAW AN OPEN MOUTH, WITH TEETH AND A TONGUE IN THE RIGHT PLACES, AS BIG AS YOU CAN. THEN IN THE MIDDLE, DRAW IN ALL OF YOUR FAVORITE FOODS TO FILL IT UP!

COMING TO TERMS

Some of the words on this page might be new to you, but they're things your body uses and does every single day!

Carbon dioxide: a gas we breathe out

Cardiac: anything that relates to the heart

Blood vessels: tubes that blood flows through

Esophagus: a tube that pushes chewed food from the mouth to the stomach

Melanin: a substance in your body that gives color to your skin, hair, and eyes

Nutrients: substances, such as vitamins, minerals, and proteins, that are needed for health and growth

Neurons: cells that receive and send signals within the body

Organs: body parts that have a job to do

Vertebrae: the bones that form the spine

FUN(KY) FILL-IN!

Now that you've learned some super serious words relating to the human body, it's time to get a little **silly**.

Make a list of nine nouns. Fill in the blanks of each sentence with the corresponding word from your list, then read the sentences out loud!

Your list:

1._____

2._____

3._____

4._____

5._____

6._____

7._____

8._____

9._____

1. _____ are the tubes that blood flows through.

2. We breathe out _____.

3. _____ is a word for anything that relates to the heart.

4. The _____ pushes chewed food from the mouth to the stomach.

5. _____ gives color to your skin, hair, and eyes.

6. _____ are cells that receive and send signals within the body.

7. _____ are needed for health and growth, and are found in vitamins, minerals, and proteins.

8. _____ all have a job to do.

9. The bones that form the spine make up the _____.

COMMON SENSES

The human body has five senses.

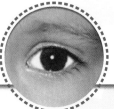

Your ability to see depends on your eyes working together.

Your sense of hearing is enabled by your ears. They can tell you whether a sound is near or far, as well as where the sound is coming from.

Your sense of smell comes from your nose, which also breathes in air.

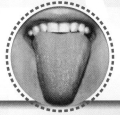

Your ability to taste comes from the taste buds on your tongue. Your sense of smell helps you taste food.

Your sense of touch is all over your body. It is in your skin.

BODY OF TRUTH!

There are five taste categories: sweet, salty, sour, bitter, and umami. Umami is sometimes called savory.

STINK FACTOR

Our sense of smell is very sensitive. Humans can identify up to 1 trillion different smells!

SENSORY PERCEPTION!

Connect the sense to the matching image by drawing a straight line from one dot to the other. Circle the letters that are not crossed out to complete all three sentences below, and learn how your brain receives messages!

Messages from the brain travel through _____ in your spine.
_____ branch out from the spine to every part of your body and then send messages back to your brain. _____ tell your brain about everything. They tell you about what you see, feel, hear, smell, and taste.

SEE

HEAR

SMELL

TOUCH

TASTE

A E N P
L I E
R E O J W
D E F
R V
O U H K X R B T G
C Y E A
M S
Q

A LOOK BACK:

We all know something catastrophic happened to kill off all the dinosaurs. But that wasn't the first time such an event had occurred. Before the Triassic period, 90 percent of the world's species were wiped off the planet.

FACTOSAURUS!

At the time of the dinosaurs, all of Earth's land was crunched together in one huge continent called Pangaea.

EORAPTOR

STEGOSAURUS

By the time the Triassic period came along, new species of plants and animals were beginning to find their place around the globe. Dinosaurs were one of those new creatures of the middle Triassic period.

TRIASSIC

252-201 million years ago
At the start of the Triassic, the world looked very different from how it looks today. Toward the end of the Triassic period, small- to medium-sized dinosaurs made their first appearance on Earth. The world was warm and dry, and the continents were beginning to split apart.

DO-IT-YOURSELF TIMELINE:

TRIASSIC

JURASSIC

WAY BACK!

The dinosaurs lived during the Mesozoic era, which is divided into three periods.

BRACHIOSAURUS

SPINOSAURUS

AMARGASAURUS

JURASSIC

201-145 million years ago

The climate became tropical during the Jurassic period. Trees, ferns, and other greenery blanketed the lands. But flowering plants and grasses had not yet started growing. This was the heyday of the dinosaurs, and it's when the biggest dinosaurs—such as the sauropods—were common.

CRETACEOUS

145 to 66 million years ago

The dinosaurs continued to thrive during the Cretaceous period. New groups such as the Ceratopsians were coming into being, and flowering plants came on the scene while Pangaea continued to break apart.

Reveal which dinosaurs lived in each period by adding the correct stickers to the timeline below!

Answer on page 95.

You'll need the **STICKERS** at the end of the book.

CRETACEOUS

CERATOPSIANS

Ceratopsians carried a headdress of horns and frills. They lived in herds during the Cretaceous period. Some walked on two legs, but they all could walk on all fours.

Their large frills and prominent horns, coupled with a large beak, gave these dinosaurs a truly out-of-this-world appearance. The large frills may have protected the dinosaur against attacks. Some scientists think that the frills might have been a way for heat to escape, to signal another dinosaur, or attract a mate.

STYRACOSAURUS

TOROSAURUS

TRICERATOPS

Like many of today's animals, CERATOPSIANS lived in herds.

DRAW A TRICERATOPS!

1. Start with an egg shape for the body and a U shape for where the head will be.

2. Add lines for the other main features: legs, tail, and horns.

3. Give shape to the head, legs, tail, and horns. Add some of the face, including the beak and an eye.

4. Add details to the main structure: toes, the skull's ridges, knees, and body.

5. Add wrinkles and shadows to make your dinosaur look realistic.

6. Color in your *Triceratops* for full effect!

FACTOSAURUS!

The *Triceratops* is one of the most recognized dinosaurs. It was the biggest of the horned dinosaurs, and was one of the last dinosaurs to become extinct.

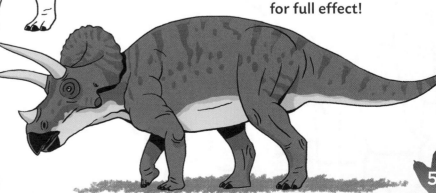

BIG AND BOLD
TYRANNOSAURUS REX

The huge *Tyrannosaurus rex*, with its powerful bite and sharp teeth, was one scary dinosaur. It was a fierce hunter. *Tyrannosaurus rex*'s arms are strangely small, but they were a lot stronger than they look.

Tyrannosaurus rex was a theropod. It was a meat eater, and among the largest dinosaurs. Some scientists think they hunted in packs, but would also eat an animal they found already dead.

FACTOSAURUS!
Theropods were quick and agile. With their big brains, they were among the smartest dinosaurs.

T. REX EFFECT!

Bring this *Tyrannosaurus rex* to life by coloring him in, however you'd like!

FACTOSAURUS!

Surprisingly, *T. rex* hatchlings may have been covered with feathers. There is still a lot to learn about this fierce predator.

THEROPOD means *"beast-footed."*

DINOS OF A FEATHER

We all know a dinosaur when we see one. We know that dinosaurs were prehistoric reptiles that lived on land. And we know that dinosaurs laid hard-shelled eggs.

But did you know that even though most dinosaurs were scaly, some dinosaurs had feathers? And did you know that dinosaurs are part of the archosaur group, which includes pterosaurs, crocodiles, and birds? Yes, birds! Dinosurs with bird-like feet were called ornithopods.

One of the links between dinosaurs and birds was probably the 150-million-year-old *Archaeopteryx*.

DEINONYCHUS
Deinonychus was a meat eater. It probably had feathers, but it could not fly.

UTAHRAPTOR
This feathered dinosaur had toe-claws up to nine inches long!

FACTOSAURUS!
Science got another surprise when tailbone fossils showed that, like peacocks, some feathered dinosaurs fanned their tail in a dazzling display to attract mates.

ORNITHOPOD means "bird-footed."

HADROSAUR
Also called duck-billed dinosaurs, *hadrosaurs* generally lived near water, had replaceable teeth, and feet like those of a giant ground bird.

FACT VERSUS FICTION!

After reading the previous page, choose which of the sentences below are true.

1. *Utahraptor* had very long toe claws.

FACT
FICTION

2. Dinosaurs laid eggs.

FACT
FICTION

3. *Hadrosaurs* kept the same teeth for their entire lives.

FACT
FICTION

4. Dinosaurs attracted the attention of mates in similar fashion to chameleons.

FACT
FICTION

5. Ornithopod means bird-footed.

FACT
FICTION

MOVING PAST THE MESOZOIC

By the end of the Mesozoic era, when dinosaurs began to disappear, the planet was getting wetter and cooler, and Pangaea was beginning to break up, creating the water and landmasses we know today.

PTEROSAURS

There were no people around when the dinosaurs were alive, but lots of other kinds of plants and animals lived back then. There were insects and small mammals. Prehistoric fish filled the oceans. Flying reptiles soared overhead.

At the beginning of the Mesozoic, there were different kinds of trees and giant ferns. By the end of the era, flowers and some grasses had emerged. There was life everywhere.

MOSASAURS

FACTOSAURUS!

Gigantic flying reptiles soared through the air, and huge, fearsome swimmers filled the seas. They may have been big and scary, but they were not dinosaurs. Dinosaurs lived on the land.

DINO DRAW!

DOODLING!

DRAW A FEW OF YOUR FAVORITE DINOSAURS HERE.

STEGOSAURUS
A REAL FASHION PLATE

Stegosaurus was as big as two rhinoceroses and had a heavy, spiked tail, and a brain the size of a golf ball. It would have been a prime target for the hungry meat eaters of the day.

The line of bony plates that stood up along *Stegosaurus's* back may have helped it control its temperature. At first, people thought these plates lay flat, like roof tiles, which is how the dinosaur got its name, which means "roofed lizard."

Stegosaurus's back was covered with plates, called scutes, made from bony material. They stood up to two feet tall and may have been used for mating or defense.

Stegosaurus may have had tough and scaly skin.

A flexible tail covered with spikes could be whipped to ward off predators.

FACTOSAURUS!
Stegosaurus fossils have been found in North America.

Shorter front legs caused *Stegosaurus's* head to be low to the ground, so they grazed on cycads and conifers.

Stegosaurus could not outrun other dinosaurs. It was a slow walker, only slightly quicker than a walking human.

FACTOSAURUS!
Stegosaurus was about 30 feet long, and weighed about 6,000 pounds!

STEGO-SCRAMBLE!

Using the facts you learned on the previous page, unscramble each of the words below and then use them to complete the sentences, and find them in the word search!

KLERWA   ORFEOD   BTEXELLF   ODSNUP   TUCESS

1. The name *Stegosaurus* means "_____ lizard."

2. This dinosaur weighed about 6,000 _____.

3. *Stegosaurus* had a _____ tail.

4. *Stegosaurus* was a pretty slow _____.

5. The plates that covered *Stegosaurus's* back are called _____.

```
I S E T U C S T D T S L R M E L
B Z V T F X R K H U C Y M E L U
J T J T R I C E R A T O P S B O
D Q J Q A S X U T P A O Z O I I
J B V S D U A V G A B A T Z X W
W E S N W S W X B H C N L O E A
K I U R O O F E D X H E Q I L L
C O K G C I S S A R U J O C F K
P M E B D X D W R P I O V U O E
M T I D Z N P K F Y D I Z B S R
S N H C H T J W Y B W L G E Q Y
```

MESOZOIC

Now see if you can find these other dino-words.

TRIASSIC   CRETACEOUS   JURASSIC

STEGOSAURUS   TRICERATOPS

Answers on page 95.

63

EXTINCTION

While scientists continue to unravel the truth about dinosaurs, they also search for the cause of the dinosaurs' extinction. How did these powerful and varied creatures get wiped off the earth?

A lot of theories are floating around to explain how dinosaurs disappeared. But there are a few facts most everyone agrees on. Climate change is one of them. Toward the end of the Cretaceous period, the climate started to cool. What caused this cooling is up for debate, though.

Evidence of an impact has experts looking to the skies. They believe that an asteroid smashed into Earth. This caused dust to blanket Earth and cool the climate. Some believe many such impacts in a very short amount of time caused the dinosaurs' demise.

One piece of evidence backs up both theories. A layer of rock from 66 million years ago is found all around the world and contains a metal called iridium.

There are two places where this metal is found. One is in Earth's core. Magma, the molten rock that spews out of volcanoes, is belched up from Earth's core. Iridium could have been carried to Earth's surface by magma. The other place iridium is found is in meteorites. Iridium could have been showered onto Earth upon impact.

FACTOSAURUS!
Triceratops was one of the last dinosaurs to become extinct.

EXTREME CLOSE-UP!

The pictures on this page are close-ups of dinosaurs you've seen throughout this section. Find each one and write down what kind it is!

1.

2.

3.

4.

5.

6.

7.

8.

Answers on page 95.

FOSSILS FOREVER

Fossils are the remains of animals preserved in the earth. If a living thing—such as a dinosaur—dies and happens to be buried in a way that keeps air, scavengers, and bacteria from getting to it, it can become a fossil.

Over time, the soft parts of the animal decay, leaving imprints in the soil, which eventually harden into stone. At the same time, minerals from the earth can soak into the animal's skeleton, sometimes preserving whole animals in rock.

FACTOSAURUS!

Paleontologists examine fossilized dinosaur teeth. Leaf-shaped, or more rounded teeth mean that the dinosaur most likely ate plants that had to be ground up. Sharp teeth mean that the dinosaur most likely ate meat and it was able to tear meat from the bone.

FROZEN IN TIME!

You've discovered a fossil, but what is it? Color in the spaces that have a green dot to reveal the shape hidden underground!

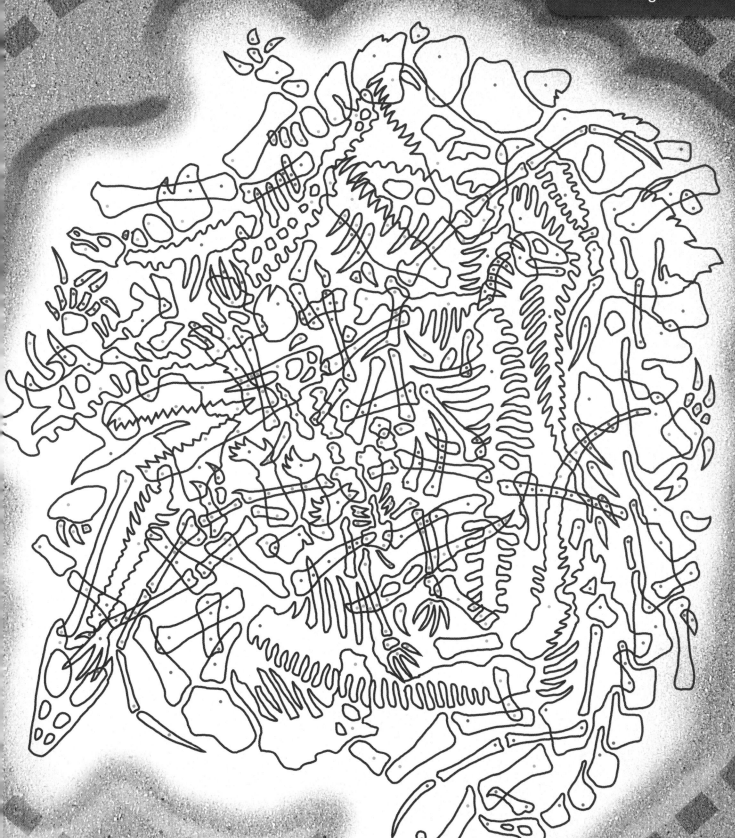

WHAT IS WEATHER?

Weather is a short-term report of the air, rain, humidity, wind, and other elements. It's what is going on in the atmosphere at any given time. Daily changes in our weather happen because of mixing warm and cool air, which can create rain, winds, storms, and more.

Weather can create an area that supports crops that will grow and ripen. But, weather can also create severe and violent conditions. Natural disasters occur from catastrophic forces of nature. Floods, hurricanes, tornadoes, earthquakes, and wildfires can change the landscape of Earth, cause damage, and put lives in danger.

WAY-OUT WEATHER!

The most rainfall ever recorded in one year is 1,042 inches in Cherrapunji, India.

WILD WEATHER!

There are many different kinds of weather—some good, some not so good! Look below, and match the type of weather to its picture by writing the correct number into the space.

1.

2.

3.

HURRICANE

BLIZZARD

THUNDERSTORM

FOG

4.

SUNNY DAY

TORNADO

5.

6.

CLOUDS: CIRRUS, STRATUS, AND CUMULUS

Clouds are made up of millions of tiny water droplets. Heat from the Sun causes water from lakes, rivers, and oceans to evaporate. This water changes into a gas, called water vapor, and enters the air. As the water vapor rises into the atmosphere, it cools, and condenses into tiny water droplets, forming clouds.

CIRRUS

Thin, feathery clouds high in the atmosphere. Usually come with nice weather.

STRATUS

Gray clouds that spread across the sky. Sometimes produce a light rain.

CUMULUS

Fluffy clouds that appear on clear days.

WAY-OUT WEATHER!

Watch out! Some cumulus clouds are cumulonimbus clouds—these towering clouds usually mean a thunderstorm is coming!

SEND IN THE CLOUDS!

DOODLING!

WHEN YOU LOOK AT THE CLOUDS IN THE SKY, SOMETIMES YOU'LL SEE SHAPES THAT REMIND YOU OF SOMETHING. MAYBE YOU'LL SEE A DRAGON OR A WHALE OR A BIG MONSTER! GRAB A PENCIL AND DOODLE SOME CLOUDS OF YOUR OWN BELOW. WHAT CRAZY SHAPES CAN YOU MAKE?

WHEN THE RAIN COMES

Rain begins as tiny water droplets in the clouds above Earth. These water droplets join together to form larger droplets and, in time, grow heavy and fall to Earth as rain.

A drizzle is a light rain that falls gently.

A downpour is a sudden, heavy rain.

A thunderstorm, though, is something else. During a thunderstorm, ice and water droplets collide in the clouds, creating electricity. The clouds discharge this electricity in the form of lightning bolts.

WAY-OUT WEATHER!

Lightning bolts are super hot! Some lightning bolts can be hotter than the surface of the Sun!

STORMY SKIES!

You can look at the clouds in the sky and see all sorts of things. But if you look at the puzzle below, you'll really see something! That's because we've hidden several things that don't belong in the storm clouds. How many can you spot?

There are

HIDDEN SHAPES!

Answer on page 96.

WINTER WHITEOUTS

Snow forms high in the atmosphere, where the air is very cold. Water vapor in the air freezes into ice crystals, which become heavy, and fall to Earth as snow. Sometimes the ice crystals join with others as they fall, forming clusters known as snowflakes.

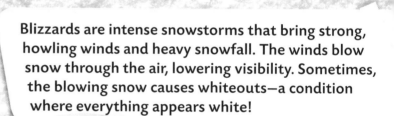

Blizzards are intense snowstorms that bring strong, howling winds and heavy snowfall. The winds blow snow through the air, lowering visibility. Sometimes, the blowing snow causes whiteouts—a condition where everything appears white!

WAY-OUT WEATHER!

No two snowflakes are the same. A scientist photographed more than 400,000 snowflakes to prove that each one is unique.

SNOW KIDDING!

It's true, no two snowflakes look alike–
except in our puzzle!

In this blowing blizzard, you'll find one snowflake that matches the snowflake shape you see here.

1.
2.
3.
4.
5.
6.
7.
8.

TORNADOES AND HURRICANES

Tornadoes come from thunderstorms, the result of strong winds that blow upward into thunderclouds. A tornado forms when this upward wind blows even faster. The winds inside the cloud begin to whirl, creating a spinning funnel cloud that stretches to the ground.

WAY-OUT WEATHER!
Sometimes tornadoes form over water. These tornadoes are called waterspouts!

Hurricanes are powerful, spinning tropical storms that bring strong winds, heavy rain, and huge waves to shore. A hurricane's winds spin around its center, or eye. The eye of the hurricane is calm, with no clouds, wind, or rain—but powerful clouds surround it.

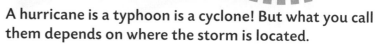

A hurricane is a typhoon is a cyclone! But what you call them depends on where the storm is located.

Hurricane: Atlantic Ocean and Eastern Pacific Ocean

Typhoon: Northwest Pacific Ocean

Cyclone: Indian Ocean and South Pacific Ocean

EYE OF THE STORM!

Hurricane winds can reach 160 miles per hour, uproot trees, crush homes, and cause massive flooding. Trust us, you do NOT want to be inside one!

But hurricane hunters fly right into them to study the storms up close! See if you can find the only safe route and make it to the eye of the storm.

Hurricane hunter aircraft

START?

START?

FINISH!

START?

START?

Answer on page 96.

CLIMATE CHANGE

The climate is a way of referring to the weather in a place over a long period of time. Earth's climate naturally changes very slowly. But recently, Earth's climate has been changing very quickly. Scientists believe this is because of human activity.

People add greenhouse gases to the atmosphere, which warm the planet. Since 1970, Earth has warmed by about 1°F. This may seem like a small change, but scientists believe it has made severe weather more intense.

WAY-OUT WEATHER!

A greenhouse gas adds carbon dioxide to Earth's atmosphere. Both driving and using electricity produce greenhouse gases.

IT'S A GAS, GAS, GAS!

As Earth's climate changes and warms, weather events can become more intense. Greenhouse gases can cause these changes.

Draw an "X" on all the possible causes of greenhouse gases below.

THE SEVEN CONTINENTS
OF EARTH

A continent is a large area of land. Generally speaking, there are seven continents on Earth. Deciding what is and what isn't a continent can be tricky. Asia and Europe aren't separated by water like the other continents, so some call this landmass "Eurasia."

Top of Earth

Asia is the world's largest and most populated continent. It makes up 30 percent of the world's total land area and is home to over four billion people.

North America

Europe

Asia

Africa

South America

Australia

Antarctica

Bottom of Earth

NATURE NEWS!

Lonely Hawaii, in the middle of the Pacific Ocean, isn't technically part of any continent at all because it was formed by underwater volcanoes.

CONTINENTAL CONUNDRUM!

It's time to test your knowledge of Earth! First, unscramble the names of the continents in the box below. Then match the names to the correct continents. Be on the lookout—some of the scrambled words aren't continents at all!

SAIA
_ _ _ _

SALATURIA
_ _ _ _ _ _ _ _ _

CTACIR LCIECR
_ _ _ _ _ _ _ _ _ _ _ _

ACRAFI
_ _ _ _ _ _

RATCANICAT
_ _ _ _ _ _ _ _ _ _

THORN CAMERIA
_ _ _ _ _ _ _ _ _ _ _ _

AHIIAW
_ _ _ _ _ _

SHOUT CAMERIA
_ _ _ _ _ _ _ _ _ _ _ _

POUREE
_ _ _ _ _ _

1.

2.

3.

4.

5.

6.

7.

GLACIERS AND ICE AGES

More than 10 percent of the land on Earth is covered in giant sheets of ice known as glaciers. Glaciers can exist only in places that get a lot of snow in the winter, but don't get enough warm weather in the summer to melt all that snow.

Glaciers can form when snow on a mountain builds up. As new snow falls, it presses down on old snow, squeezing it together and forming ice. The pressure of the ice on the rock melts a thin layer of the bottom of the glacier—just enough to allow the glacier to start to slide. Ice is heavy, and, on a sloped mountain, the ice will begin to move downward.

NATURE NEWS!

An ice age is basically a long period of cold climate around the world. Right now, we are living in an ice age that started three million years ago!

ICE AGE MAZE!

For this puzzle, we've put you right in the middle of icy Antarctica! If you want to make it back home where it's warm, you've got to go through this maze. But watch out for the glaciers! They'll sneak up you.

START!

FINISH!

Nature

NATURAL WONDERS

Earth is full of natural wonders: Fiery volcanoes, beautiful waterfalls, mysterious mountains, and colorful forests. But there are some natural wonders that deserve special mention.

THE GRAND CANYON

LOCATION: Arizona, United States

The Grand Canyon is a steep-sided canyon that has been carved from rocks by the Colorado River. The Grand Canyon is 6,093 feet deep and 277 miles wide and is one of the most recognizable landforms on Earth.

MOUNT EVEREST

LOCATION: In the Himalayan Mountain Range on the border of China and Nepal

Mount Everest is the size of almost 20 Empire State buildings—that's over 29,000 feet tall! It's the tallest mountain in the world and almost 60 million years old.

THE GREAT BARRIER REEF

LOCATION: The Coral Sea, off the northeastern coast of Australia

Made up of 2,900 separate coral reefs, the Great Barrier Reef is the world's largest reef system and the largest living structure in the world. It is so big, it can be seen from space! It is home to a wide range of sea life, including sea turtles, giant clams, seahorses, sea snakes, stingrays, sharks, and more.

SOMETHING'S FISHY!

DOODLING!

Many different kinds of fish call the Great Barrier Reef their home. But have they all been discovered? Doodle a crazy new kind of fish of your own invention!

NATURAL LANDSCAPES

A biome is a large ecosystem where plants and animals live in a certain type of climate. The climate of a region determines what plants will grow there and what animals will inhabit it. The plants and animals of each biome have traits that help them survive in their particular biome. Earth has many varied climates and biomes.

CHAPARRAL

SAVANNA

FORESTS

DESERT

GRASSLANDS

Here, and on the next page, you'll see examples of some of these biomes. Their climates range from cold (tundra) to warm in the summer, cold in the winter (taiga).

Animals such as the arctic fox have adapted to live in the tundra by changing the color of their fur to match either the cold, snowy conditions or slightly warmer summer foliage.

TUNDRA

NATURE NEWS!
Summer in the tundra only lasts between 50 to 60 days.

BIOME, SWEET BIOME!

You'll need the **STICKERS** at the end of the book.

Below, you'll see some photographs of various biomes from around the world. Your mission: Figure out which animals would live there! Take a look at the pictures, and read the clues. Then stick the correct animal on each biome. Good luck!

CLUE
It's so hot here, an animal would have to slither underground during the day to stay cool.

DESERT

ALPINE

CLUE
This herd animal is a natural mountain climber and is used by people to carry supplies.

RAINFOREST

TUNDRA

CLUE
Some very colorful animals, birds, and amphibians call the rainforest home.

FORESTS

CLUE
This animal appears to have a white coat, but its actual hairs are clear.

CLUE
Most forest animals are camouflaged with their surroundings so they blend in and can escape capture.

TAIGA

GRASSLANDS

CLUE
There are no trees or shrubs here, so this animal needs to run very fast to avoid predators.

CLUE
An animal of a different stripe loves living in the taiga.

Answers on page 96.

UNDERGROUND MYSTERIES

A cave is a natural underground space made by flowing water that wears rock away. Over time, the water will carve a path through the rock. After a very long time, this path can be big enough for a person to enter. Lots of flowing water and a lot of passing time can make for some pretty large and amazing caves.

Stalactites are formations that hang from the ceilings of limestone caves. As water drips from the ceiling of a cave, it leaves behind traces of calcite, which slowly build up until the calcite takes the shape of an icicle.

The calcite drips that fall on the cave floor build up into a long tower, called a **stalagmite**.

Stalactites

Stalagmites

NATURE NEWS!
The world's largest cave system is the Mammoth Cave in Kentucky. It is 348 miles long!

GOING BATTY!

No, your eyes aren't playing tricks on you. Below, you'll see two nearly identical images. But wait! The second picture has 10 differences from the first. Grab your gear and head into these caves to spot the differences.

EARTHQUAKES: SERIOUS SHAKES

Many massive slabs of rock on Earth's crust fit together like puzzle pieces. Each of these pieces is called a tectonic plate. Tectonic plates are constantly in motion. They shift, slide, and bump into each other. The movement of the plates against each other causes the earth to shake violently, creating earthquakes.

An earthquake feels stronger if you're closer to its epicenter. The epicenter is the point on Earth's surface at the center of the earthquake. A large earthquake may be felt hundreds of miles away from its epicenter.

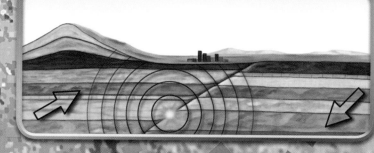

NATURE NEWS!

More than 500,000 earthquakes occur each year. Most earthquakes last for less than a minute. Many can barely be felt. But more intense earthquakes may trigger landslides, tsunamis, volcanic eruptions, and other natural disasters.

THE RICHTER SCALE

is used to rate an earthquake's power from 1 to 10.
1 = very weak
5+ = destructive

SHAKY GROUND!

An earthquake just struck our puzzle!

Using the clues below, see if you can figure out where the epicenter of this particular 'quake is located.

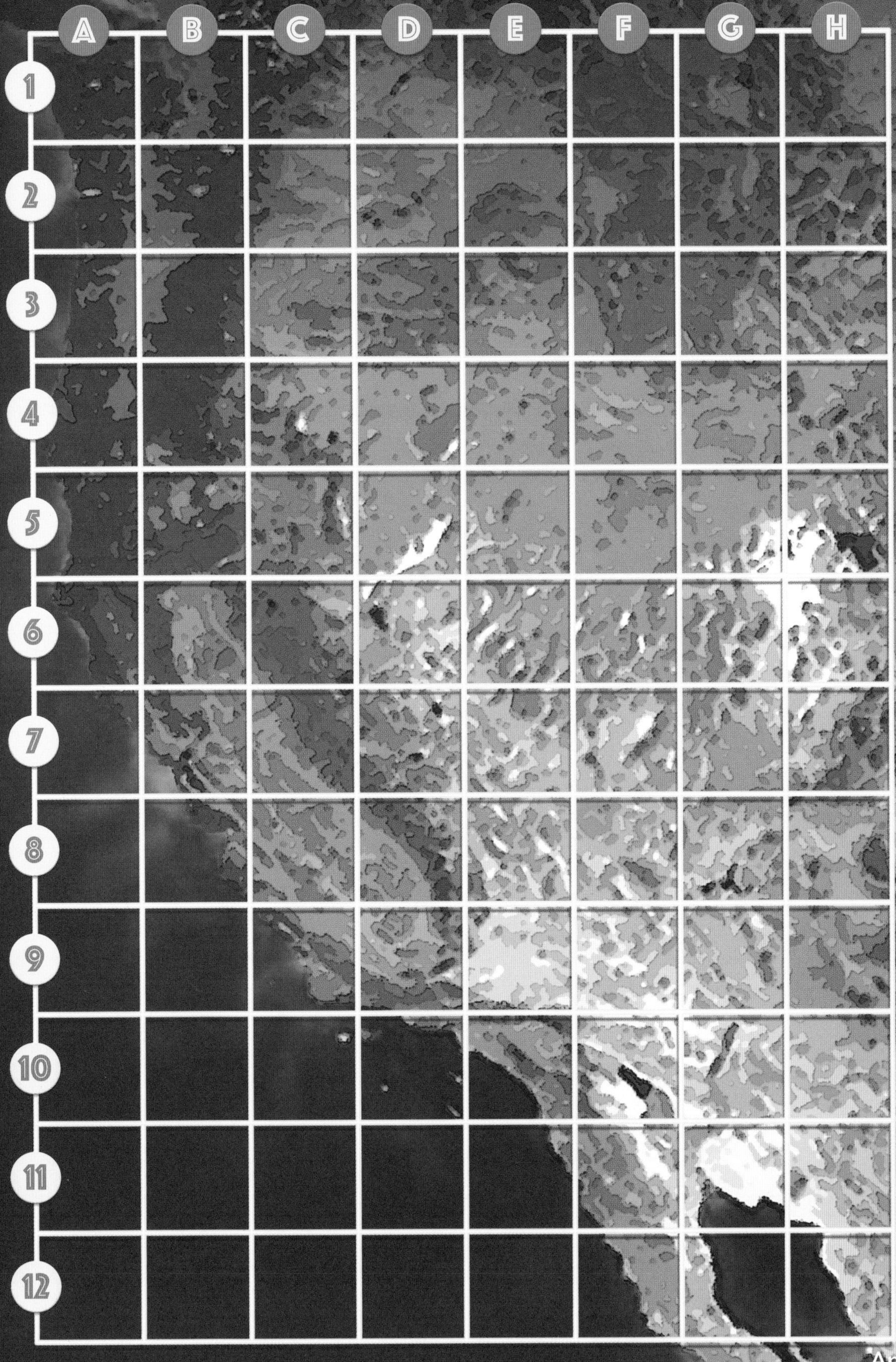

CLUES:

- Start at coordinates F1.
- Move south 6 squares.
- Move west 2 squares.
- There's some rumbling up north; move 2 squares in that direction.
- The seismograph shows activity 3 squares west.
- Move south 3 squares.
- The epicenter is 2 squares to the east.

Answer on page 96.

VIOLENT VOLCANOES

A volcano is a vent in Earth's crust that erupts ash, lava, and gases into the air. Volcanoes usually look like dome-shaped or cone-shaped mountains. Lava and ash build up over many years to create these mountains.

Beneath Earth's crust is the mantle. The mantle is so hot that it melts rock. The melted rock moves up toward Earth's surface. The liquid rock flows out of a volcano as lava!

NATURE NEWS!

Over 1,500 active volcanoes dot Earth's surface. About 75 percent of these are in the Ring of Fire in the Pacific Ocean. The Ring of Fire is formed by the boundaries of tectonic plates. Like earthquakes, volcanoes usually form where plates bump against each other.

MOLTEN MYSTERY!

One of these volcanoes is about to erupt—but which one?

To find that out, you'll need to use the clues below. But hurry up! One of these volcanoes is about to explode!

CLUES:

1. The active volcano is located near a forest.
2. There is no water near the active volcano.
3. There's a mountain right next to the active volcano.
4. There's no snow on top of the volcano.

1.

2.

3.

4.

5.

6.

Answer on page 96.

Puzzle Answers

PAGE 5:

PAGE 7:

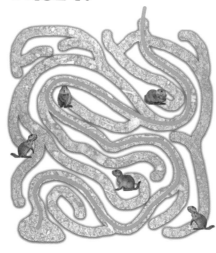

PAGE 9:

```
H V X D Q D K N V Q Y Y Q H V
C T D N I E Z U H P A N E D T
J A O J K U E N L N I A X K Y
R V S L S O Y A T H G E P H J
E A P S S U T L P X O F T I K
D U R C O Y G L A S S F R O G
P O T A P W O A M I A P A R A
A J P U B D A S N K Q Y P W X
N A S Q R Y U R I A H N X O O
D K K E E P P P Y K R D T A L
A N V M Y C F A V I U W X H O
G I N T P I C A C G V U H S T
R K L U W J Q U O H Y S L A L
X A R E D P A N N A L I N A L
P I C D T Q G B X Y Z K Z N A
```

PAGE 11:
The matching scorpion is **4**.

PAGE 15:
There are **37** zebras.

PAGE 23:

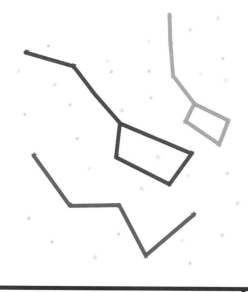

PAGE 25:

1. a
2. a
3. a
4. a
5. They're roughly the same, surprisingly!

PAGE 27:

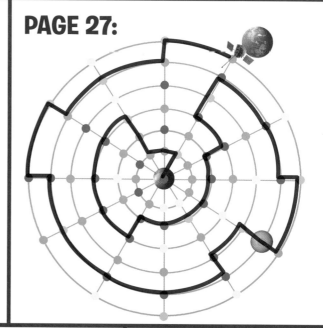

PAGE 31:

PAGE 33:

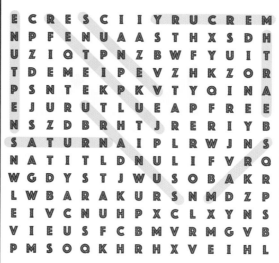

```
E C R E S C I I Y R U C R E M
N P F E N U A A S T H X S D H
U Z I Q T P N Z B W F Y U I T
T D E M E I P E V Z H K Z O R
P S N T E K P K V T Y Q I N A
E J U R U T L U E A P F R E E
N S Z D B R H T J R E R I Y B
S A T U R N A I P L R W J N S
N A T I T L D N U L I F V Q
W G D Y S T J W U S O B A K R
L W B A R A K U R S N M D Z P
E I V C N U H P X C L X Y N S
V I E U S F C B M V R M G V B
P M S O O K H R H X V E I H L
```

PAGE 35:

PAGE 43:

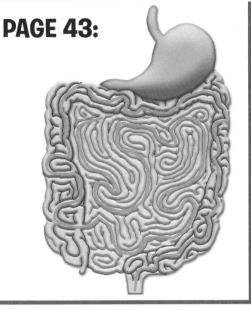

PAGE 51:

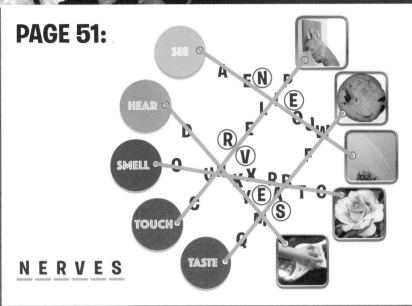

N E R V E S

PAGE 52-53:

PAGE 59:

1. FACT   **2.** FACT   **3.** FICTION   **4.** FICTION   **5.** FACT

PAGE 63:

WALKER   ROOFED   FLEXIBLE   POUNDS   SCUTES
KLERWA   ORFEOD   BIEXELLF   ODSNUP   TUCESS

1. The name *Stegosaurus* means " ROOFED lizard."
2. This dinosaur weighed about 6,000 POUNDS .
3. *Stegosaurus* had a FLEXIBLE tail.
4. *Stegosaurus* was a pretty slow WALKER .
5. The plates that covered *Stegosaurus's* back are called SCUTES .

```
I S E T U C S T D T S L R M E L
B Z V T F X R K H U C Y M E L U
J T J T R I C E R A T O P S B O
D Q J Q A S X U T P A O Z O I I
J B V S D U A V G A B A T Z X W
W E S N W S W X B H C N L O E A
K I U R O O F E D X H E Q I L L
C O K G C I S S A R U J O C F K
P M E B D X D W R P I O V U O E
M T I D Z N P K F Y D I Z B S R
S N H C H T J W Y B W L G E Q Y
```

PAGE 65:

1. *HADROSAUR*
2. *STYRACOSAURUS*
3. *TYRANNOSAURUS REX*
4. *MOSASAUR*
5. *STEGOSAURUS*
6. *DEINONYCHUS*
7. *EORAPTOR*
8. *SPINOSAURUS*

PAGE 67:

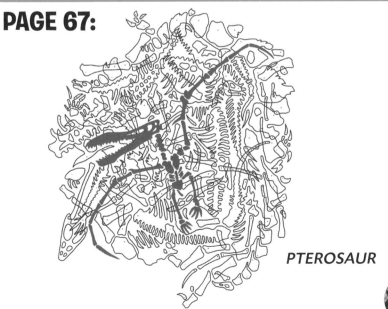

PTEROSAUR

PAGE 69:

1. FOG
2. TORNADO
3. THUNDERSTORM
4. HURRICANE
5. BLIZZARD
6. SUNNY DAY

PAGE 73:

12 hidden shapes

PAGE 75:

The matching snowflake is 6.

PAGE 77:

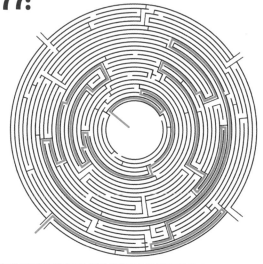

PAGE 79:

PAGE 81:

SAIA
<u>ASIA</u>
SALATURIA
<u>AUSTRALIA</u>
CTACIR LCIECR
<u>ARCTIC CIRCLE</u>
ACRAFI
<u>AFRICA</u>
RATCANICAT
<u>ANTARCTICA</u>
THORN CAMERIA
<u>NORTH AMERICA</u>
AHIIAW
<u>HAWAII</u>
SHOUT CAMERIA
<u>SOUTH AMERICA</u>
POUREE
<u>EUROPE</u>

1. SOUTH AMERICA
2. NORTH AMERICA
3. ANTARCTICA
4. ASIA
5. AFRICA
6. EUROPE
7. AUSTRALIA

PAGE 83:

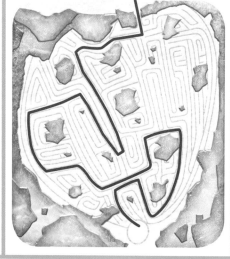

PAGE 87:

PAGE 89:

PAGE 91:

The epicenter is C8.

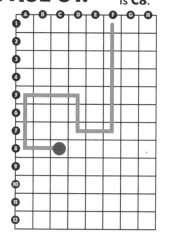

PAGE 93:

The correct volcano is 4.

VENUS

EARTH

JUPITER

MARS

URANUS

SATURN

NEPTUNE

MERCURY

PAGE 52-53 - DO IT YOURSELF TIMELINE

PAGE 87 - BIOME, SWEET BIOME!

SIBERIAN TIGER

BISON

RATTLESNAKE

OPOSSUM

LLAMA

RED-EYED TREE FROG

POLAR BEAR

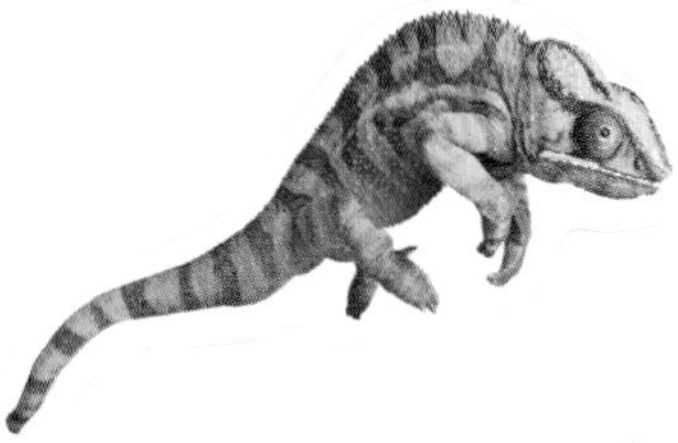
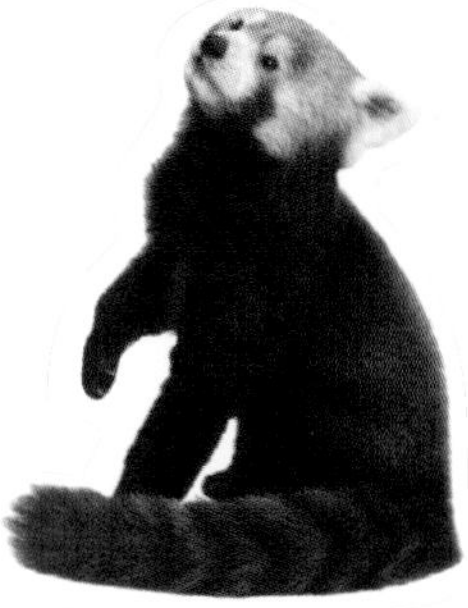
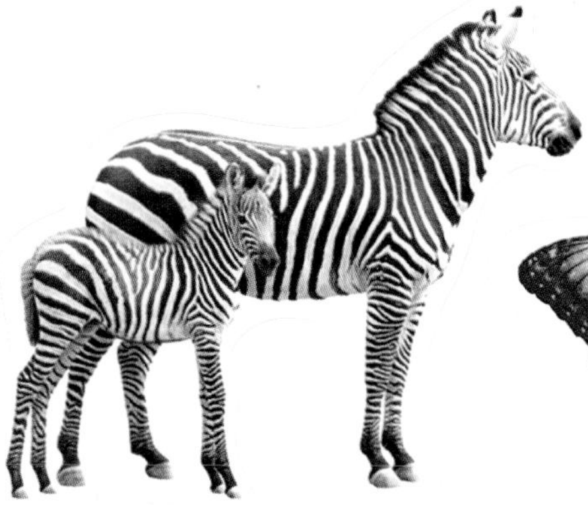
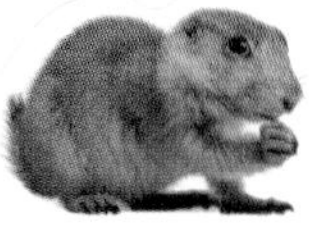
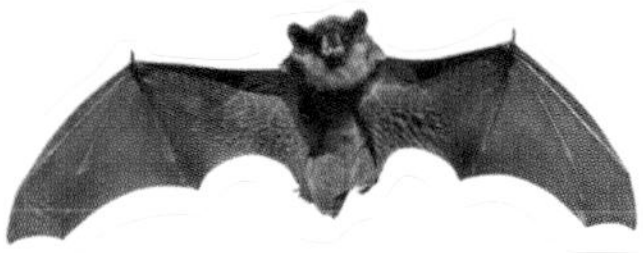
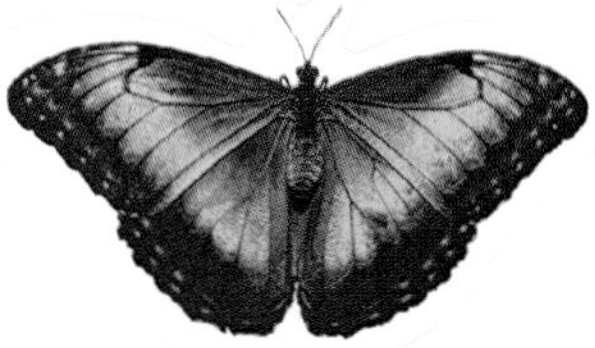
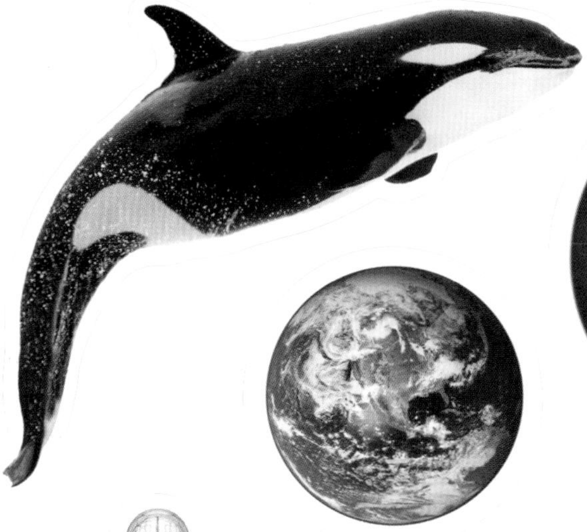
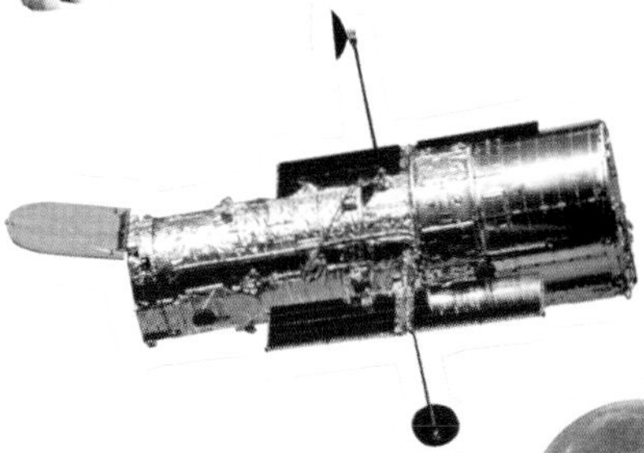
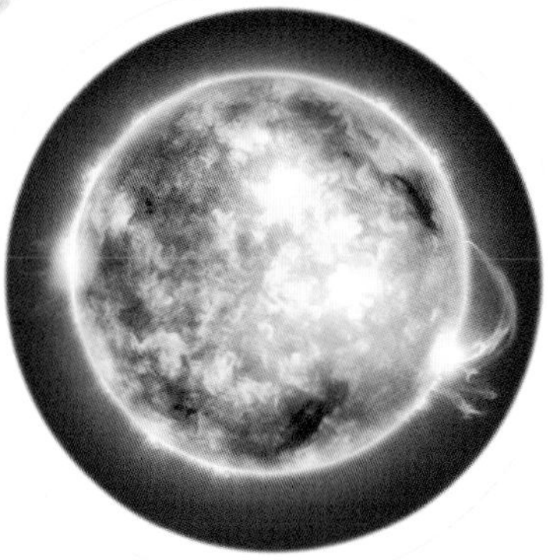
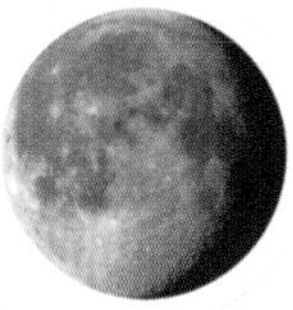
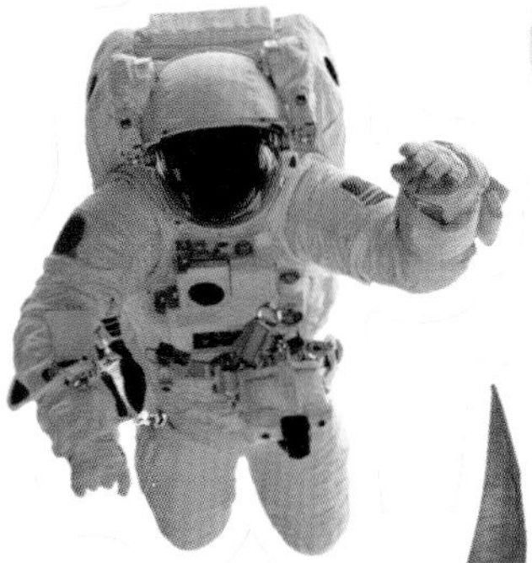
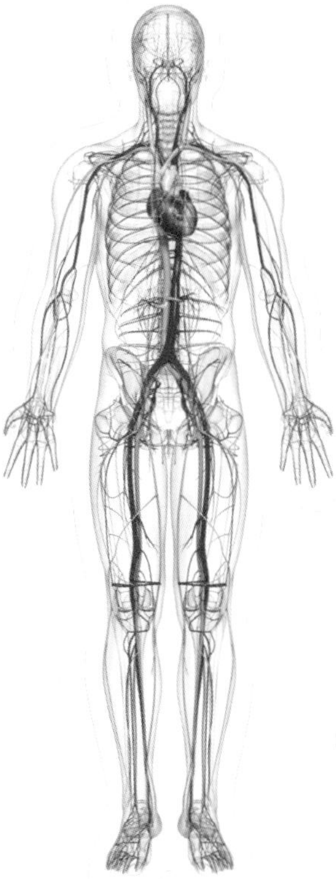
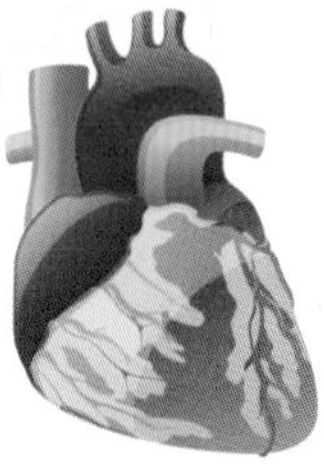
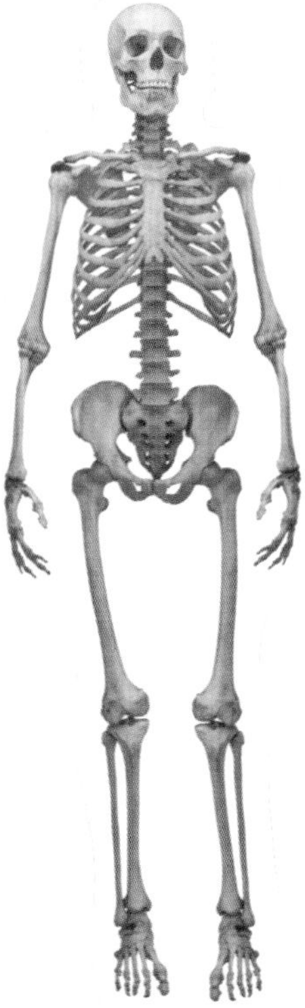
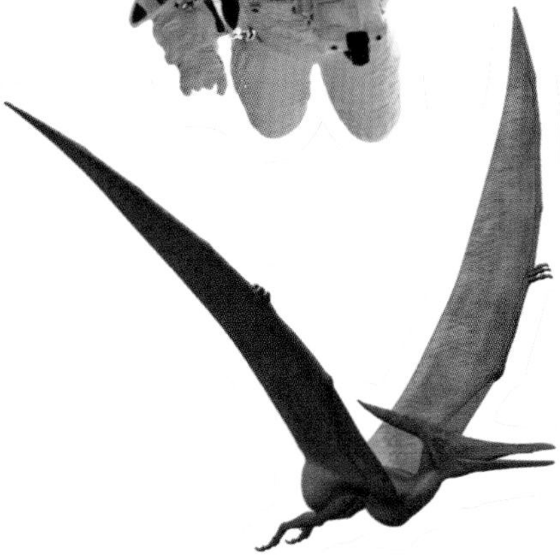
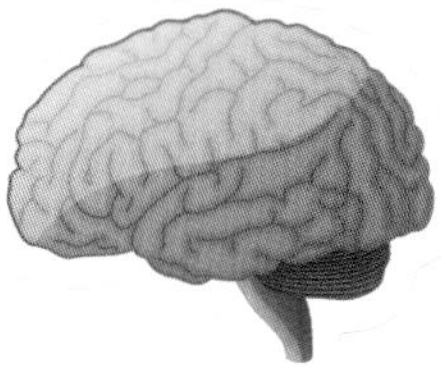
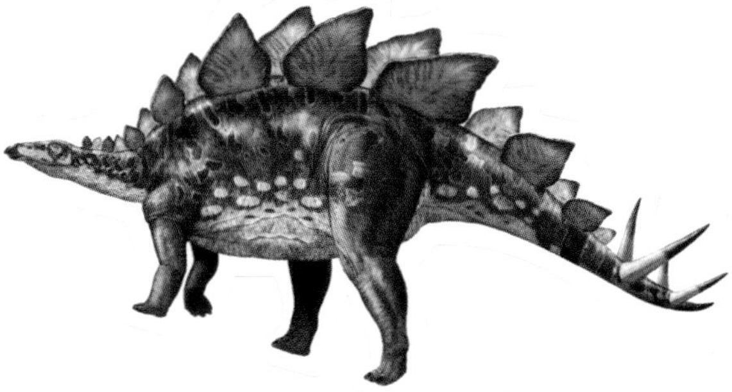
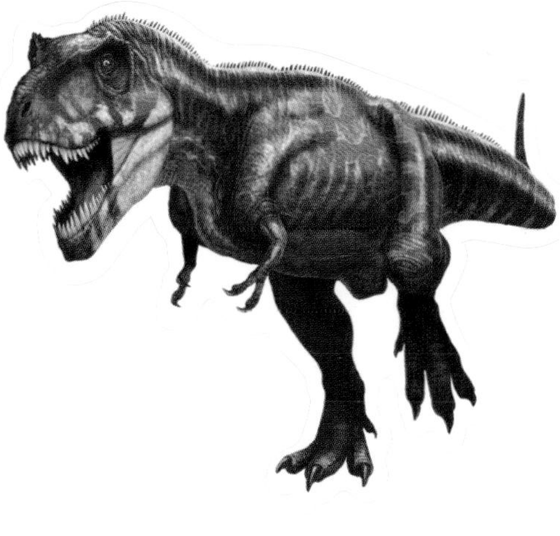
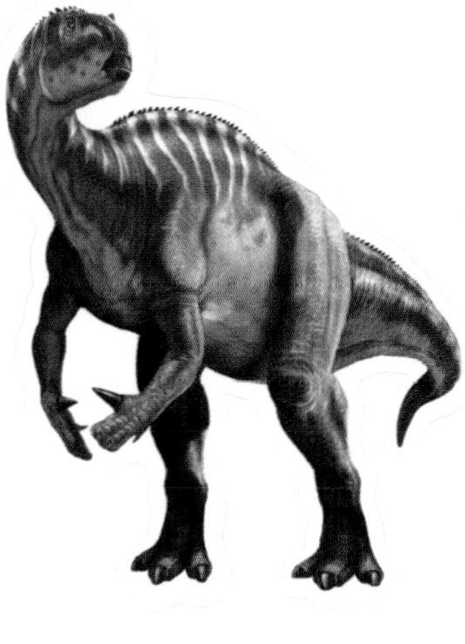
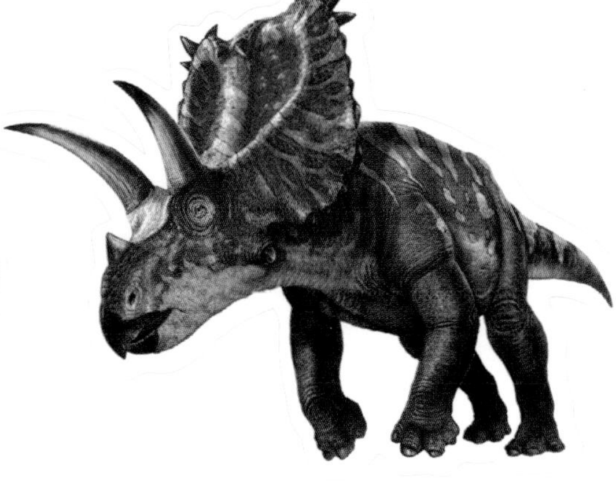

OUR SOLAR SYSTEM

JUPITER

MARS

EARTH

VENUS

MERCURY

SUN

EARTH'S MOON

Length of day:
29.5 Earth days

Length of year:
27 Earth days

Average distance from Earth:
238,900 miles

Diameter at equator:
2,159 miles

Surface details:
Rocky, with hills, mountains, and craters

Made of:
Partly molten core may be metallic iron, sulfur, and nickel; crust of mostly oxygen, silicon, magnesium, iron, calcium, and aluminum

Temperature:
−387°F to 253°F

EARTH

Length of day:
24 hours

Length of year:
365.25 Earth days

Average distance from the Sun:
92,900,000 miles

Diameter at equator:
7,926.28 miles

Number of moons:
1

Surface details:
About 70% is covered with water and 30% is land with rock, soil, and plants

Made of:
Core of mostly nickel and iron; crust of a mixture of minerals

Average temperature:
57°F

VENUS

Length of day:
243 Earth days

Length of year:
225 Earth days

Average distance from the Sun:
67,000,000 miles

Diameter at equator:
7,521 miles

Number of moons:
0

Surface details:
Hot, dry rolling plains, with large lowlands, two large highlands, some mountains, and craters

Made of:
Central iron core with a rocky mantle

Average temperature:
864°F

MERCURY

Length of day:
59 Earth days

Length of year:
88 Earth days

Average distance from the Sun:
36,000,000 miles

Diameter at equator:
3,030 miles

Number of moons:
0

Surface details:
Rocky planet with ridges, cliffs, and craters

Made of:
Huge iron core with a rocky mantle

Temperature:
−279°F to 801°F

SUN

Age:
4.6 billion years

Rotation time at equator:
26.8 Earth days

Rotation time at poles:
36 Earth days

Diameter at equator:
864,938 miles

Number of orbiting planets:
8

Surface details:
Ball of burning gases without a solid surface; different parts rotate at different rates

Made of:
92.1% hydrogen, 7.8% helium

Temperature:
27,000,000°F at the core